Future-Proof Selling
The Salesperson's Guide to Adaptation and Innovation in a Rapidly Evolving World

By Stuart William Pattison

Table of Contents

Introduction

I have been in direct sales and a Sales Leader for over 35 years. At the end of each year, I pause to reflect upon he past 12 months, taking stock of results. As I do every year I work to set goals for the new year, I always consider what I need to change and what obstacles I must overcome to reach new heights.

This year has been especially insightful, as I have taken a sabbatical from leading teams and moved back into direct sales. This is a significant change for me and it is providing a fresh perspective and revealed numerous opportunities for improvement. Though I miss the camaraderie of my team, this transition into direct sales has pushed me in positive ways - keeping me driven, adaptable, and open to self-examination. I am sharpening the saw. What is very clear is that the changes ahead will require all salespeople to push deep into their discomfort to be able to adapt to changes that are truly significant and if you are a salesperson you need to be aware and prepare or risk failure.

I am eager to share the lessons I have learned and help establish clarity around the evolving need for purpose and set new priorities. By building on my decades of experience while exploring uncharted territory, I aim to end this transitional year with focus and vision for what is next. This introspective period has prepared me for the new year with renewed passion, creativity, and commitment to raising the bar. The sales profession faces an unprecedented pace of technological, economic, and social change as we enter 2024. From Artificial Intelligence automation to TikTok selling and generational shifts redefining B2B relationships, the turbulence looks unlikely to slow. Salespeople anchored to legacy practices will find the future increasingly eluding their grasps.

This book charts a course of understanding to help salespeople work to adapt and thriving through the chaos sweeping sales instead of becoming overwhelmed reacting to forces out of control. By upgrading perspectives, tactics, and tools for the modern context, individuals and teams sustain high relevance and performance amidst the churn. Signature resilience and persuasion skills so innate to sales now meet their biggest challenge yet to adapt - or fade away as buyer options multiply exponentially.

The time for conservative incremental improvement has clearly passed. The following chapters detail a transformation imperative for sales in 2024 through upgraded skills, processes, and strategies. The bottom line is salespeople now need a more tech-savvy, data-driven, flexible and customer-centric approach compared to traditional techniques. Mastering these changes will set them up for sales success in the years ahead.

Change always marked sales roles with shifting product lines, competitor plays, and customer needs requiring constant responsiveness. But the blistering pace of technological, social, and economic evolution today categorically differ. AI automation, global connectivity, and breakthrough innovation compound daily, each enabling unprecedented new consumer experiences and business models.

These exponential forces combine into a virtual tsunami threatening to overwhelm sales teams clinging to past decades paradigms. Handling lead pipelines developed for analog means falters processing internet-augmented buyers. Physical field selling limits reach amid mobile messaging lifestyle shifts. Intuition-led pursuit misfires against data-savvy committee decisions.

Survival demands shedding outdated constraints and comfort zones before the tsunami of change sweeps them away for good.

Sales originations must pressure test each element of strategy, process, technology, and culture against extreme scenarios of plausible futures. Where can emerging innovations improve conversions? What parts of the sales experience can virtualize? How could augmented decision intelligence redirect ineffective efforts?

This book navigates these questions toward building truly future-proof sales functions. But progress requires first acknowledging the extent of revolutionary change barreling down upon sales roles. The future is already here - it is just unevenly distributed.

Let the journey begin...

Chapter One - Adopting digital and social selling strategies

After over three decades in sales and sales leadership roles, I've seen my fair share of changes in the field. But the rise of digital and social selling over the past 5-10 years has truly marked a seismic shift in the sales arena. As both a seasoned pro and admitted digital novice, I knew I needed to challenge myself to adapt to this rapidly evolving landscape regardless of what roll I play at any company.

At first, I stubbornly clung to the sales fundamentals and practices that had made me successful thus far. Cold calls, warm leads, attending networking events, centers Of Influence development, and consultative deal-making - these were my bread and butter. But as many of my loyal clients retired or companies shifted budgets increasingly online, I couldn't ignore the writing on the wall any longer.

With humility, curiosity, and determination, I am gradually immersing myself in digital sales tools and social platforms. I attended conferences and trainings, experimented with LinkedIn outreach and drip campaigns, working with Google Analytics, posting for the first time on LinkedIn, and enlisted my son's help in decoding TikTok and other social trends.

The learning curve has been steep at times and mistake-ridden for sure. Just when I feel like I'm getting the hang of Instagram Stories and keeping up with LinkedIn, there seems to be some new AI-powered sales technology I need to wrap my head around. But I'm encouraged by small wins, like forging new connections through niche Facebook groups and boosting visibility with targeted content creation.

While I still have so much to learn, adopting these digital and social strategies has kept me adaptable and challenged me to expand my skillset - qualities that benefit me and my clients. My journey reminds me that wisdom and openness to change can cross generational divides in this fast-moving marketplace. I may never become an expert in all the latest tech, but I strive to balance my old-school relationship building with new tools that push me in the right direction.

With more buyer journeys happening online, salespeople need to get comfortable utilizing digital tools like LinkedIn, webinars, and social media to connect with prospects. Cold calling alone won't be enough anymore. People don't answer the phone or respond to a creative voicemail anymore. E-mails get lost or deleted. Stopping by someone's office or place of business is considered rude.

I started my career as a stockbroker tied to an automatic dialing machine and making well over 300 cold calls a day. The stereotype of salespeople endlessly making cold calls from dusty boiler rooms misses how selling has evolved. Increasingly, buyer journeys play out digitally across search, social media and more before ever connecting with a rep. To stay relevant, modern salespeople must complement traditional tactics with digital and social approaches such as the use of LinkedIn.

LinkedIn is the social media platform most commonly used by B2B marketers and their clients worldwide. LinkedIn continues to update and change their algorithm. LinkedIn's ultimate goal is to prioritize relevant, high-quality content and promote engagement. With increase use and crafting connections in the application the better the algorithm will promote you. The LinkedIn algorithm aims to prioritize relevant content and promote engagement. LinkedIn supports content that will get the most likes and shares and automatically set to show you 'Top' content and most popular topics.

Here are some key tips that will help increase your profile and posts:

- Optimize Profile: Fully complete all details
- Create Engaging Content: Use relevant hashtags, tag others, add emojis. Increase interactions by liking, sharing, commenting and reposting. Post consistently when your audience is most active. Provide detailed opinions and commentary.
- Use Visuals: Add images, videos, infographics.
- Optimize Headlines: Use keywords aligned to your expertise to create clear, interesting headlines.
- Participate in Discussions: Join active conversations.
- Build Your Brand: Promote your community, interests and expertise authentically.
- Expand Reach with Ads: Use LinkedIn Campaign Manager to reach more users.
- Keep Content Strong: Share clear, interesting, engaging content.
- Follow Aligned Leaders & Companies: Connect with those that mirror your interests and expertise.

By optimizing your profile, creating engaging content, and expanding your reach, you can increase the visibility of your LinkedIn posts and build a more robust, active network. LinkedIn's unmatched professional data and continuing centrality make it a must for sales. It's an updatable rolodex that can easily grow and connect you to targeted professionals that would otherwise be difficult to reach. It's a verifications that you have experience and can add value.

Creating Targeted Ads and Promotions
- Run LinkedIn Sponsored Content showcasing your best assets.
- Retarget high-potential site visitors with customized ads.
- Create nurture journeys specific to their profile and interests.
- Track performance data to optimize future campaigns.

- Dialed ads keep you and your company's brand and offerings top of mind and differentiate from your competition.

Along with the uses on websites and social media work to connect with you clients, contacts, prospects, and leaders in the industry by conducting Webinars, lunch & learns, hosting networking events, happy hours, and Virtual Events.

Here are some examples to engage prospects:
- Host educational webinars with industry guest speakers
- Run virtual conferences, meetups and networking events
- Record on-demand content for those who can't attend live
- Promote registrations through email, social media and outreach
- Add in social connectors like ski trips, social events, sporting events
- Use webinars to position yourself as a trusted advisor.

Leveraging Social Selling
- Share valuable insights daily on networks like Twitter and Facebook…
- Respond to discussions and questions from your followers.
- Join relevant communities and conversations on social media.
- Ensure your social bio links back to your sales materials.

Social establishes your product and category expertise.

While relationships and the very basics of selling retains importance like building rapport, uncovered needs, building trust, lessoning, offering targeted solutions and customer service need to be upheld, the digital touchpoints increasingly influence the buyer's journey. Combining traditional relationship building with an omnichannel digital approach makes success inevitable.

The stereotype of pushy salespeople peddling product features is obsolete. Modern buyers have too many options and do their own research. To earn their business, position yourself as a trusted advisor focused on providing value, rallying around their needs, and demonstrating tangible ROI.

Developing relationships in this new world is critical, but you must Sell Value, Not Just Features.

Buyers suffer "feature fatigue" trying to compare solution capabilities. Wowing them with speeds and feeds fails. Instead, you must sell around value:
- Identify the customer's operational and business objectives.
- Illustrate how your solution helps achieve those goals.
- Quantify the financial value such as increased revenue or cost reduction.
- Compare against alternatives to demonstrate superior value.

This elevates you from product pusher to strategic consultant. Being an advisor and simplifying value and individualizing your approach will create more wins.

Provide Complete Solutions

Instead of isolated point solutions, customers want integrated platforms spanning their end-to-end needs. Satisfy their thirst for simplicity through:
- Determining all aspects of the customer's workflow
- Offering or connecting complementary solutions across their stack
- Becoming the one-stop orchestrator across modules
- Ongoing support adapting as their needs evolve over time

Fulfilling more needs builds stickier and more profitable relationships and solid retention of a portfolio of clients.

Obsess Over Demonstrating ROI (Return on Investment)

Financial return on investment remains the ultimate proof point for B2B buyers. Crisply illustrate ROI by:
- Calculating direct cost reduction or profit increase
- Identifying process and operational efficiencies gained
- Determining payback period until positive return
- Quantifying downstream impacts like improved customer retention

Back up claims with data models, benchmarks, and case studies. Buyers invest in ROI, not features.

As both an experienced sales pro and admitted digital novice, I knew embracing digital selling was critical to stay relevant. Here are the ten tactics delivering massive impact for me:
- Build an impressive LinkedIn profile highlighting my expertise to strengthen my personal brand.
- Run customized LinkedIn ads tailored to different high-value buyer segments I target.
- Create targeted video content around specific customer pain points for YouTube and social media.
- Send new prospects personalized video messages via email or SMS introducing myself and value I provide.
- Set up Google alerts for key target companies and contacts to instantly notify me of developments and news.
- Upload educational presentations to SlideShare and promote them to my target verticals and contacts.
- Add capability overview microsites personalized to each of my top service offerings.

- Automate lead follow-up and nurturing by integrating my CRM (Customer with marketing automation.
- Build tailored email templates for outreach to different stages and buyer profiles using AI copywriting tools.

By aligning your problem-solving capabilities tightly to customer goals, operationalizing end-to-end solutions, and quantifying financial outcomes, you become an indispensable growth catalyst steering their business success. Sell around that!

Chapter Two - Leveraging Artificial Intelligence

Here are just a few statistics to help you understand how AI is hyper-changing the business world as we know it:

- By 2022, 60% of organizations are expected to be using AI to assist human workers.
- AI could contribute up to $15.7 trillion to the global economy by 2030, boosting business productivity by up to 40%.
- Over 50% of business leaders say AI will allow them to obtain or sustain a competitive advantage.
- 89% of business leaders believe AI will significantly alter or transform their industry in the next 5 years.
- By 2024, AI identification of risks and opportunities could potentially result in an additional $9.1 trillion in business value created.
- 63% of IT leaders say AI automated tasks and processes is the main business driver for AI adoption.
- 80% of emerging technologies in business will have AI foundations by 2022.
- Over 75% of commercial enterprise apps will use AI by the end of 2023.
- Natural language processing and predictive data analytics, both AI-powered, will drive business innovation, especially in marketing and sales.
- AI in business is projected to grow from $1.4 billion in 2018 to $59.8 billion by 2025, an impressive 42.8% compound annual growth rate.
- Interest in building AI Websites has increased by 50% in the last year
- The Global AI Market is expected to increase by 37% each year from 2024 to 2030

When I first heard about AI (Artificial Intelligence) I really just ignored it. I'll admit - I was skeptical that it was a big deal. As a sales leader who had done pretty well relying on my own personal approach for over a decade in the banking industry, I didn't see how some high-tech software was going to help me or my team. Surely my many years of experience and honed intuition would trump some fancy algorithms?

However, with adoption being accepted and a little understanding and now used daily, I dove in - and my eyes were and continue to be quickly opened to the potential. As I added connections and fed more data into my sales assistant dashboard, what I thought was just a gimmick started surfacing truly useful insights. The tool can predicting my hottest leads, analyzing past deal cycles to forecast close dates, and even recommending custom messaging to improve open and response rates.

As the adoption of AI across my competitive peer group is slow and many of my peers hesitant about the technology, I have leaned hard into the AI understanding as a competitive advantage. I set up custom alerts for major account moves, automated tedious administrative work, and used the suggested content for my tougher prospects. My email open rates had never been higher and I can firmly credit my sales assistant for helping me break into multiple new strategic accounts.

Now when anyone asks me about leveraging these emerging AI technologies, I tell them bluntly - lean into it. It is an amazing tool and a true game changer. While it takes some adjusting and has limitations, I've been blown away by the value-add. I never anticipated artificial intelligence would play a meaningful role in sales, but the data and support it provides has become indispensable. I urge all salespeople - don't let the unknown hold you back. Embrace the future that is already here with AI. You'll be shocked at what it can unlock for accelerating your pipeline and revenue growth.

As a salesperson navigating the rise of artificial intelligence, I see ample opportunities to utilize AI to boost my productivity and exceed targets. While some view AI as threatening to replace sales roles, I believe machine learning will become my secret weapon if applied strategically. The key is understanding where AI can best support me across the sales process.

For example, many CRMs now provide AI lead scoring to gauge the potential of inbound prospects based on historical data patterns. Instead of manually sifting weak leads, I can focus calls and emails only on AI-verified premium opportunities personalized to each client's profile. Further, virtual assistants can help you quickly gather relevant intel to customize pitches and nurture sequences.

When combined with human creativity and emotional intelligence, AI elevates my consultative skills instead of replacing them. You can use chatbots to handle basic inquiries while directing freed bandwidth toward building rapport with high-value accounts. I also lean on AI for ongoing recommendations to keep target prospects warm across channels until they convert. I use it to write unique e-mail to capture a prospect's attention.

While AI won't replace the need for sales expertise, failing to adopt it will make any seller less effective over time. By smartly applying AI to supplement my strengths, I can accomplish more than I could achieve alone. That's why continuously improving through AI will be essential for salespeople to exceed quotas in such a competitive climate. The time to leverage these innovations is now if I want to dominate as an individual producer long-term.

Here are some very specific, actionable ways a salesperson can utilize AI right now to drive sales growth:

- Use AI writing assistants to generate initial email outreach templates for each targeted prospect category. Tailor these starting points to craft personalized messages faster.
- Build custom intent classifiers so AI chatbots can effectively screen incoming leads and route the most promising ones to your queue.
- Create dynamic video sales pitches powered by AI copywriting and natural language generation tailored to each client's company and needs.
- Integrate speech recognition and analytics into sales calls so virtual assistants can transcribe discussions and highlight insightful talking points for future reference.
- Input notes from past deals won and lost into machine learning platforms so AI can determine what factors influence close rates for your offerings.
- Automate data entry and contact logging with AI data assistants to eliminate post-call administrative tasks so you can connect with more leads per day.
- Use conversational AI platforms to run through objections and develop rebuttals you can deploy in the moment during sales negotiations.
- Generate hyper-targeted digital ads for your most valuable services using AI ad copywriting scaled across multiple platforms.
- Tap predictive lead scoring models to reveal lookalike target companies with ideal buyer profiles to focus immediate prospecting efforts.
- Schedule meetings automatically by using AI assistants to identify mutually compatible times across participants based on past calendar history.

AI is here and has tremendous benefits. Work to learn, use and adapts and the growth in production, efficiencies and increased time to time with prospects and clients will be immeasurable.

Artificial intelligence is transforming the sales landscape. AI technologies like machine learning, natural language processing, and predictive analytics are creating new opportunities for salespeople to boost productivity, efficiency, and revenue growth.

While some may view AI as a threat that could replace human jobs, the reality is that AI is most powerful when combined with uniquely human strengths. The savvy salesperson will embrace AI as an invaluable asset to complement their creativity, emotional intelligence, expertise and vision.

Specifically, AI can handle rote administrative tasks, screen and route leads, provide data-driven insights, and generate customized messaging and content at scale. This empowers salespeople to focus on building relationships, understanding client needs, overcoming objections, and closing complex deals.

The bottom line is that failing to continually educate yourself on emerging AI will put any salesperson at a huge disadvantage. Lean into and learn about new innovations. Experiment with implementing AI tools across your workflows. The salespeople who effectively blend their intuitive abilities with AI stand to gain a dominant edge over the competition and exceed targets.

While AI adaption has some challenges, the benefits for supercharging sales ability and achievements far outweigh any obstacles. Make the commitment to utilize AI as your new secret weapon if you want to maximize your personal production and career growth well into the future. The time to leverage these tools is now.

Chapter Three - Building Relationships on Through Social Video

When I took over a new sales team, connecting with prospects on social media seemed awkward. But as buyers shifted online, I adapted. I focused on value, not promotion, consistently showing up and delivering helpful content. By embracing social platforms to effectively scale relationships, I developed strong bonds that generate more qualified leads than analog channels alone.

Social selling is now imperative, but many salespeople limit themselves to aging platforms like Twitter and LinkedIn. With consumer attention rapidly shifting, ambitious teams must expand reach across emerging social video channels as well. Messaging platforms likewise enable authentic relationship building at scale.

Engaging Through Video

Many sellers still just blast promotional content with little personalization. Modern social selling requires genuine engagement. As audiences fracture across apps, salespeople must actively participate in conversations through video comments, responses and dialogue.

Commenting meaningfully on prospects' videos builds familiarity and trust at scale. Educational and entertaining formats avoid hard sells, establish expertise, and seed future relationships.

Video Tips for Sales Professionals

The key for success in social video is providing value. Humanize your brand by introducing team members and highlighting company culture. Share relevant tutorials, "day in the life" job footage and industry trend explainers suited to your audience's pain points.

Keep videos concise at 1-2 minutes for optimal mobile viewing and retention. Use simple editing software to incorporate brand assets. Monitor comments and respond thoughtfully when appropriate to spark ongoing dialog.

Measure views, completion rates and engaging questions as key performance indicators versus vanity metrics like clicks or followers. Refine content over time based on feedback and demonstrated buyer interests.

Chat Apps Enable Genuine Dialog

Messaging platforms like SMS, WhatsApp and WeChat also warrant inclusion to smooth eventual sales transitions. Their intimacy enables trust building through genuine back-and-forth conversation at scale.

With exponentially expanding digital touchpoints, sales professionals must inject helpful perspectives early and consistently across multiple social video channels rather than just traditional business platforms. This always-on selling approach drives deeper buyer familiarity and relationships to boost revenue results.

Chapter Four – The future of Sales Excellence

The future sales person needs to provide consultative value, not just transactions. Become an insightful advisor guiding customers to solutions. Master this advisory approach and the future looks bright.

Building a strong center of influence network is incredibly valuable for salespeople to generate leads, referrals, and advice for sales success in the future.

A few years ago I took over a new team in commercial banking sales, I thought it was all about pitching products and closing deals. But I quickly learned how much the sales landscape was changing. Buyers expected more – they wanted a true advisor who understood their business needs and guided them to the right financial solutions.

I knew I needed to take a more consultative approach. So I focused on asking questions, listening, and truly identifying the core challenges my prospects faced. By researching their industries, I could make informed recommendations tailored to their unique situations. Sometimes that meant suggesting solutions beyond just what I was selling. My goal was to solve their problems, not just make commissions. I also realized that in today's digital world, leveraging technologies and networks leads to sales success. I tapped into my centers of influence – accountants, lawyers, consultants who worked with prospects that could benefit from my services. Rather than cold calling, I nurtured referral relationships over months and years. And I embraced sales technologies to work smarter – using CRM to capture every client interaction, testing sales messaging, publishing helpful thought leadership content online. While the tools were new to me, dedicating time to master them gave me a competitive edge. Throughout it all, I stayed focused on genuinely helping clients and adding value however I could. My consultative, customer-first approach built trust and loyalty. I ended up with the best reward – raving fans who were enthusiastic references and sent streams of referrals.

The future buyer has higher expectations. By continually providing exemplary service and adapting to changes in the industry, I've developed all the capabilities for sales success now and in the years to come. Though the solutions I offer will evolve, providing consultative value will always be the key.

The sales landscape is shifting. Buyers today are more informed, connected, and empowered than ever before. To thrive in this environment, sales professionals must adapt by providing true consultative value and guiding customers to the best possible solutions. This chapter outlines key strategies for sales excellence now and into the future.

The business world is changing rapidly, and sales approaches need to evolve to stay successful in the future. You need to be fulling prepared with a pre-call plan before meeting any high-level prospect. Here are my top tips for adapting your sales approach:

- From features to solutions. Don't just pitch product features, focus on understanding customer problems and challenges. Then suggest customized solutions that directly address their needs.

Become a problem-solving advisor.

- Data-driven insights. Leverage data like never before - sales analytics, customer relationship data, market research reports, etc. Identify trends and growth opportunities. Use insights to refine sales targeting and messaging.

- Consultative questioning. Ask intelligent, probing questions to uncover customer pain points. Listen attentively to fully understand motivations and context. Tailor pitches accordingly.
- Educational marketing. Position yourself as a thought leader sharing valuable insights vs a sales rep pushing products. Publish helpful content and have informed discussions.
- Relationship networks. Leverage networks, referrals and social media much more for sales leads and advice. Connect on LinkedIn and nurture relationships over time.
- Tech fluency. Embrace technologies like AI to enhance productivity. Use tools like CRM, automation and analytics to gain efficiencies and customer insights. Know basic digital selling techniques.

Building a Value-Driven Approach

The days of transactional sales pitches are over. Customers expect more. They want a trusted advisor who deeply understands their needs and guides them to the ideal solutions, not just the products with the best commission. By taking a consultative approach focused on value, salespeople become indispensable partners to their clients.

Some best practices include:
- Asking thoughtful questions to uncover root causes and context behind customer needs.
- Conducting research to develop industry and client insights that suggest better solutions.
- Presenting customized recommendations tailored to each client's unique situation.

- Maintaining follow-up dialogs to continue adding value after the sale. Here are some top tips:
- Identify ideal connections. What types of professionals regularly interact and advise your potential clients? Common options are lawyers, accountants, consultants, executives, industry thought leaders, etc. Target 5-10 centers of influence to build relationships with.
- Provide value upfront. Don't just ask for referrals or favors right away. Offer helpful insights, articles, and tips first to build goodwill and demonstrate your expertise. Nurture relationships over time.
- Attend industry events. Conferences, association meetings, and trade shows provide exposure to well-connected influencers. Make time for relationship building conversations. Follow up afterward to continue dialogs.
- Build referral partnerships. Eventually, work directly with centers of influence to formalize referral partnerships. Agree to introduce each other to potential new clients that seem like a good mutual fit.
- Expand connections through centers of influence. Ask who else they may recommend connecting with through warm introductions. Aim to build a network wheel vs just straight sales pipeline.
- Maintain consistent communication. Continue providing periodic value to centers of influence like insider industry articles or invite them to relevant webinars. Check-in from time to time.
- Approach building a center of influence network as forming win-win partnerships versus just transactional sales relationships. Demonstrate long-term interested in adding value however you can.

The most successful salespeople put solving customer problems above all else. They earn loyalty and referrals by providing exemplary service.

Expanding Centers of Influence

Leveraging networks is critical for driving more qualified leads today. Rather than cold calling, sales professionals should focus on building strong referral partnerships. Identifying well-connected professionals who interact with your potential clients allows you to organically build relationships and credibility. Over time, they are happy to introduce you to prospects who may benefit from your services. Target individuals like executives, consultants, lawyers, accountants and industry thought leaders. Initially focus on providing them value through helpful insights and information. As you build goodwill, formalize referral partnerships where you mutually agree to connect each other with promising new contacts. A large network of centers of influence who actively refer new business to you can transform your sales pipeline. Adapting Techniques for the Digital Age. Rapid technology advances demand new sales capabilities. Artificial intelligence, sales enablement tools, customer analytics and digital communications channels are reshaping best practices.

Some key areas to focus on include:
- Leveraging customer data and insights to deeply understand motivations.
- Testing sales messaging content to refine value propositions.
- Building educational thought leadership content and social media connections.
- Using tools like CRM to track all customer interactions and analytics to quantify results.

As selling goes digital, tech fluency is no longer optional. The most successful sales professionals embrace new techniques and use them to their advantage.

Remember to Focus on consultative value and customer service, which remains vital even as sales evolves.

- Leveraging modern tools and networks is mandatory to stay competitive But the best salespeople balance that with an intrinsic drive to solve customer problems
- By internalizing a customer-centric ethos and upholding high support standards, sales mastery sustains
- While surface-level strategies may shift, the principles of care and needs-based solutions are timeless
- Through genuine customer partnerships, sales professionals can excel now and in the future

The future buyer demands more. They expect salespeople to progress beyond features to provide real solutions. By becoming customer-focused trusted advisors, sales professionals future-proof their success. Those who adapt to emerging trends in networks, service and technology selling will thrive.

As the sales world evolves, the core foundations for excellence remain anchored in value, service and relationships. While sales professionals must stay adept in utilizing modern tools and strategies, what sets the truly exceptional ones apart is their dedication to understanding customers and solving real problems. By internalizing a consultative mindset and upholding robust standards of support, salespeople future-proof their success. They become trusted advisors who guide buyers to the right solutions, foster loyal advocates and enjoy prosperous careers built on referrals. While outwards tactics may change with the times, at its heart sales mastery stems from making each customer feel genuinely cared for and putting their needs first. By living these principles, sales professionals can thrive amidst any disruption.

Chapter Five – Building your own Personal Branding

I still remember feeling on top of the world as I passed my goal in connections on LinkedIn earlier this year. And now as one of newer sales reps at my firm, I am investing tremendous work into expanding my network and reinvent myself as a expert in the insurance industry. I am working to differentiate myself by building my own brand in support of the company I promote. I realized early on that digital networking was going to be pivotal for sales success even in the traditional direct B2B domain.

From painstakingly sending personalized invites to cold calling connections of in-market prospects, my inbox flooded daily with new contact requests. Alongside, I leveraged content to establish myself - publishing regular LinkedIn posts and guest articles that highlighted my perspective on challenges faced by my customer base of COIs and current contacts.

The effort is starting to pay off as I became a familiar name among the decision maker crowd in my target market. My insights received enough traction to opportunities at marquee invited to networking events and industry conferences. And most importantly, the swell of relationships translated into an overflowing sales pipeline as industry players proactively reached out for solutions.

So when that LinkedIn connection counter flipped to a higher level, I took it as external validation that my personal brand building is creating succuss. In my mind, it cemented my status as a recognized thought leader and set me apart from the average sales rep grinding it out. However, the euphoric high faded quickly when I reflected back on what exactly those connections represented.

Was more connections meaningful to building new relationships that knew me for the value I brought? Had the majority even engaged deeply enough with my content to grasp my perspective and experiences that shaped my personal brand? If not, what was the worth of connections collected like trophies rather than intentionally nurtured professional relationships? I have focused so intensely on expanding my network that I had failed at actually improve my networking focus.

The lesson I am learning is that a personal branding requires authentic relationship building as the foundation, not vanity metrics. While tools like LinkedIn enable expanding visibility and access faster, you need to leverage them to drive understanding of your differentiated value. Not all LinkedIn connections hold equal weight when individuals invest their precious time into building trust with you rather than merely clicking a button. As I course corrected my outreach strategy accordingly, I realized quality always overrides quantity when establishing any brand - personal or otherwise.

The business world is undergoing rapid changes as we enter 2024. The world as we know it has shifted. Its hard to get my head around why everything seems so different, but it a new game. Emerging technologies like artificial intelligence, automation, and virtual reality are disrupting traditional ways of working across all industries. Consumer preferences and buying patterns are shifting as new generations with different values and priorities take center stage. Combined with uncertainties in the global economy, this makes for a volatile and unpredictable environment for sales professionals.

To thrive amidst the turbulence, developing a strong personal brand as a salesperson has become more critical than ever. Your personal brand essentially communicates what unique value you bring to customers and sets you apart from the competition. As executive attention becomes an increasingly scarce resource, having a recognizable and defined personal brand gives you an edge in accessing key decision makers. Equally importantly, it fosters trust and loyalty amongst existing clients.

Buyers today are more informed and self-educated. Or at least they think they are and that google information and simplify solutions. To engage them effectively, you need to position yourself as an industry thought leader rather than just another salesperson. This means actively sharing your perspectives and insights on major industry challenges through platforms like LinkedIn, podcasts and trade publications. Make predictions for the future of your industry. Dedicate time to crafting a coherent point of view that brings value to your customers.

Here are a few tips to help you build your brand:
Here are top tips I would include in a chapter to help salespeople build their personal brand:

- Define Your Niche and Areas of Expertise - Determine the specific industries, products, services and buyer personas you want to be known for
- Create Consistent Taglines and Bios - Craft short, memorable taglines and bios highlighting your niche expertise to use across platforms
- Provide Value Through Educational Content - Share posts, articles, videos, etc. that provide tangible value for your ideal prospects
- Show Personality and Behind-the-Scenes Access - Give a glimpse into your life and personality to become relatable
- Interact Frequently and Helpfully - Reply to comments, questions and messages in a timely, thoughtful manner

- Develop Referral Partnerships - Team up with complementary providers to endorse each other's brands
- Claim Your Name on Key Channels - Secure social media handles, domain name etc. for your name to strengthen brand
- Track Brand Signals and Metrics - Follow brand mentions, engagement, traffic drivers to guide content
- Consistency Counts - Maintain steady visibility through an ongoing content cadence
- Make Improvements Over Time - Leverage feedback and results to continually refine brand messaging

Showcase subject matter expertise.

As products and services get increasingly complex, customers look for sales reps with specialized knowledge of their needs. Make sure to consistently exhibit your expertise of your customer's business issues on social channels and client conversations. Invest time in upskilling yourself on market trends, emerging technologies and solutions relevant to your field through online courses, conferences and networking events. Let your expertise shine through. You need to be an expert in your industry, but you also need to be well versing into those you are calling on.

Leverage the power of content.

Content and social selling have become indispensable elements of sales strategy today. Maintaining an active blog, securing speaking opportunities at events and leveraging platforms like Instagram and LinkedIn are great ways for showcasing thought leadership. Combine educational content with lifestyle posts that give a peek into your personality to build authentic connections with buyers. Video content is especially powerful - consider creating a YouTube channel highlighting your perspective on industry challenges.

By proactively working on these personal branding efforts, sales professionals can thrive even in volatile markets. A strong personal brand inspires confidence in your value and serves as a key differentiator. It also future-proofs you against disruptions caused by new technologies and buyer behaviors. So whether a rookie getting started in sales or a seasoned expert, now is the time to work on leveling up your personal brand!

Chapter Six - Leveraging data and analytics

I've been in sales since the mid 1980's and I've seen a lot of changes in the industry over that time. When I first started out, sales was very much about personality and persuasive skills. We relied on cold calls, networking, and working our personal connections to land deals. Data and analytics just weren't a major part of the job.

But over the last several years, I have seen sales transform with the rise of new technologies and the availability of more data. Now more than ever before, leveraging the data and making metrics-driven decisions is critical to success in sales. I learned this lesson the hard way a few years back when my team was struggling to meet my targets for the year.

No matter how many calls we made or meetings booked, we just weren't able to move the revenue needle as much as I knew we were capable. When I took a step back to analyze what was going wrong, the data told the story – my team just wasn't targeting the right companies or people. Once I started digging into the analytics on our client base and target market, I moved the team to change their focused actions and we were able to refine refocus. I realigned our outreach and pitches based on key data like company revenue, growth trends and customer lifetime value. Almost immediately after I revamped the strategy guided by the data, my numbers started to improve and we ended up surpassing out targets for the year.

Now data and analytics forms the foundation of my own sales process. Whether it's shaping my prospecting lists based on key attributes or figuring out how to close more deals by understanding sales cycles - I am leveraging data to guide my decisions and actions. While personality and relationships still matter tremendously in sales, combining that human touch with data-driven insights has been a total game changer. My team's performance reached new highs ever since embracing analytics as an integral part of excelling in sales.

There's more customer and sales data available now. Salespeople should learn to leverage CRMs, sales analytics, buyer persona information and other data to gain insights that help tailor pitches better.

The datafication of sales opens tremendous potential. Salespeople now access expansive datasets around customers, performance trends, market movements, and more. Leveraging analytics helps tailor your messaging, optimize processes, and win more deals. Follow these best practices:

Mine Your CRM and Marketing Data

Modern CRMs and marketing automation platforms contain goldmines of intelligence. Unearth insights by:
- Building detailed buyer persona profiles based on demographics and attributes.
- Analyzing deal trends across customer segments to guide resource allocation.
- Identifying cross-sell opportunities based on complementary purchases.
- Triggering automated nurture campaigns matched to individual activity.

Segment and structure all this data for personalization at scale.

Track Sales KPIs (Key Performance Indicators) and Analytics

Monitoring metrics helps diagnose performance issues and showcase your value. Prioritize tracking:
- Sales cycle length by offer to optimize funnel velocity.
- Win rates for forecasting and managing capacity.
- Recurring revenue to showcase customer loyalty.
- Activity volume like calls and emails for rep productivity.

Surfacing trends arms you to improve processes.

Apply Insights to Messages and Pitches

The maximal customization enabled by analytics only realizes value when applied to actual selling situations. Use data to:
- Tailor pain point messaging to each customer's specific challenges.
- Reference cohort benchmarks or trends to make figures tangible.
- Predict lifecycle stage to match content to their mindset.
- Recommend add-ons based on complementary purchase data.

Informed by insights, your messages feel personalized and prescient.

Combine digital elevation of relationships with human creativity and strategy. Sales is now an analytics-powered craft.

The datafication of sales has ushered in an era of tremendous potential for salespeople. As this chapter has shown, leveraging data analytics allows you to optimize processes, personalize messaging, forecast more accurately, and ultimately win more deals.

The key is tapping into the insights buried within the mass amounts of customer, performance and market data now available. Build detailed buyer personas. Continuously analyze win rates, deal cycles, and other sales KPIs. Use these findings to trigger targeted campaigns, address pain points, and showcase your value.

While relationships still form the heart of sales, injecting data and analytics into your workflows elevates outcomes to new heights. Combining digital precision with human creativity and strategy creates an unbeatable edge.

The future of sales belongs to professionals who embrace analytics across the entire revenue engine. To stay ahead of the competition and maximize your commission, dedicating yourself to translating insights into impact is now mission-critical. Turn available data into increased performance. Become an analytics-powered master of your craft. The time is now to leverage metrics to sell smarter.

Chapter Seven - Customizing outreach for different audiences

I have always focused on relationship deepened and differentiation and giving every potential client the consistent same generic pitch. I had a standard pitch deck I would march through about our company and products, rarely deviating from the script. My team's close rate was good, but my team and I struggled to stand out and connect with our leads. I trained every sales rep to be consistent, and we would roll-play the story and work on consistency. Our sales meeting had become boring and repetitive, but we had our pitch locked and loaded.

Once I started customizing the entire pitch to match each industry, integrating terminology they would relate to and use cases specific to that type of business closing new business grew. I would maneuver to match their priorities like streamlining complicated regulatory reporting - and proposed tailored solutions based on their needs.

It taught me a critical lesson - taking the time to deeply understand my different audiences and customizing my outreach is essential. Whether it is spinning up industry-specific collateral, integrating a customer's language, or tailoring a demo - I now shape my entire approach to each prospect's situation. My conversion and win rates have shot up dramatically thanks to focusing on truly connecting with what matters most to each customer. Though time-intensive on the front end, customization pays off exponentially in sales cycle velocity, size of deals closed, and partnership with accounts.

With Gen Z and Millennials making more B2B buying decisions, sales approaches need to resonate across generations. Personalized, authentic connections are key. The business world as we knew it has shifted and as salespeople we need to match the changes Infront of us to be successful as we move into the new year.

The one-size-fits all sales pitch no longer resonates in an increasingly fragmented market. Buyers range from traditionalists clinging to old school interactions to digitally native millennials and Gen Z blazing new purchasing paths. Adapt your style to connect by:

Appealing to Traditional Buyers

Long-time incumbents still control major corporate decisions. Cater to their preferences with:
- Whitepaper collateral explaining capabilities in detail.
- Consultative 1:1 calls focused on relationship building.
- In-person events like golf outings and happy hours.
- Executive briefing centered presentations.

In sectors skewing older, time-tested tactics still prevail.

Engaging Younger Buyers

Digital native decision-makers entering the workforce desire flashier and more convenient selling. Meet them by:
- Creating visually engaging and bite-sized content.
- Leveraging chatbots and interactive tools.
- Sharing behind-the-scenes looks at company culture.
- Publicizing values and social causes important to them.

This sense of purpose and personality appeals more than old formalities.

Blending Both Worlds

Diverse buying committees featuring veterans and newcomers bridge these styles. Orchestrate hybrid outreach combining:

- Thought leadership and credibility markers from traditional sales.
- Authentic storytelling and interactive tools expected by younger buyers.
- Omnichannel mix of in-person, phone, digital, and self-service.
- Emphasis on genuine relationship building across demographics.

Atomic precision targeting and mass personalization drives modern success.

While core values persist across audiences, outreach presentation matters greatly. Customize your interface to align with how different buyers like to engage while retaining strategic consistency. Meet buyers where they are now rather than where you want them to be. This balancing act allows you to thrive across any account.

The diversification of the B2B buyer means salespeople can no longer rely on a one-size-fits-all approach. As discussed in this chapter, tailoring your outreach and messaging to connect with different generations and personas is now essential to succeed.

Traditionalists still wield significant influence in many industries and respond best to time-tested tactics like whitepapers and golf outings. Meanwhile, digitally-savvy millennials and Gen Z desire interactive content, authentic branding, and self-service tools.

The key is blending these styles for hybrid teams. Maintain core consistency in your strategy, while customizing the outreach presentation and interface. Get the best of both worlds by conveying thought leadership and relatable showcasing company culture and values. Meet veteran buyers where they prefer through consultative calls. Engage younger buyers by highlighting social causes and leveraging chatbots.

The bottom line is that precision targeting and personalization now drive sales excellence. Take the time to understand your diverse audiences and tailor approaches accordingly. Salespeople who customize outreach to align across demographics will forge more genuine connections. They will also outperform those clinging to commoditized pitches in our increasingly fragmented business landscape. Become a sales chameleon and adopt the mindsets of those you engage. This balancing act holds the key to thriving across any account in the modern age.

Chapter Eight - Aligning with marketing and customer success teams

I have managed teams and been a leader in direct selling for many years and, I'll admit – I was always selfishly focused on just my and my team's numbers and pipeline. As long as I was hitting my quotas and budget and my boss or board was pleased, I didn't pay too much attention to the other teams or even the competition. But a couple deals earlier this year that unexpectedly fell apart taught me that sales can no longer operate in a silo.

I lost a seemingly solid prospect because while the lead came from a top CIO I though was an easy close, we didn't have long-term data about the fit or expected lifetime value that the customer success team tracks. On another deal, a lack of communication with the solutions architects led to confusion about timelines and project scope that soured the customer. Shifting industries and moving to direct sales has had me reinvent myself and adapt to the new world of selling. Having a focus on delivery value to a prospect is critical.

These were tough lessons, but they have inspired me that you need to build tighter bridges across departments. I now meet regularly with our marketing team to share feedback on campaign performance and collaborate on high-value segments to target. I also looped customer success earlier into deals to set reasonable rollout expectations. Suddenly with this enhanced alignment, my deals started moving smoother and faster.

The biggest wake-up call early this year at my former company came when I was preparing for a large enterprise renewal. Customer service sent me in-depth analytics on the client's usage and satisfaction over the past year. I discovered they weren't fully utilizing key product capabilities that could solve pressing pain points. Armed with insights from Customer service analytics, I presented a customized roadmap focusing on high-ROI features. My cross-team alignment directly won us that lucrative renewal and an expended business relationship.

Now cross-functional transparency and strategy alignment is becoming second nature to me. Whether reviewing campaign metrics, mapping product adoption targets, or setting retention goals, I firmly believe collaborating across teams is the recipe for sales success today. Though initially jarring, adapting to this teamwork approach has exponentially grown my career.

Sales no longer happens in a vacuum. Closer collaboration with marketing for lead generation and post-purchase customer success activities is crucial.

An outdated view of sales, marketing, and customer success as separate silos hurts revenue and retention. Customers expect consistent messaging and experience throughout their buying journey – no matter the department. Modern sales leaders synthesize their work across teams by:

Collaborating With Marketing

Smooth hand-offs between marketing and sales require close collaboration. Work together by:
- Providing feedback on lead scoring and content strategy.
- Comparing inbound vs outbound channel effectiveness.
- Crafting coordinated multichannel nurture campaigns.
- Jointly building an ideal customer profile model.

Shared KPIs like pipeline generation and velocity encourage collaboration in the buyer's best interest.

Coordinating With Customer Success

Post-purchase is the new pre-sale. Customer success drives critical retention and expansion revenue. Align by:

- Introducing customers early to set usage expectations.
- Analyzing churn predictors to resolve at-risk accounts.
- Communicating unique customer needs for better onboarding.
- Updating product teams on desired feature requests.

This closed-loop system optimizes fit and value realization.

Breaking down departmental barriers lands more deals and nurtures their long-term growth. Adopt a customer-centric structure based on buying lifecycle rather than functional domains. This amplified alignment maximizes lifetime value.

Modern sales leaders recognize that operating in departmental silos no longer drives success - cross-functional transparency and strategy alignment across marketing, sales and customer success is now essential. By collaborating across teams, sharing key performance metrics, and crafting unified buyer experiences, salespeople can smooth hand-offs, retain more customers, and maximize lifetime value. The future belongs to sales organizations that embrace an aligned, customer-centric structure focused on the entire buying lifecycle.

Chapter Nine - Virtual Sales Calls

If you told me even just three years ago that I'd soon be conducting the majority of my sales meetings virtually, I would have laughed. Before covid it was not a common way to communicate externally. In my decade in strategic enterprise sales, I had cultivated a process relying heavily on wining-and-dining prospects and reading body language to close million dollar deals. Yet seemingly overnight in early 2020, in-person touchpoints vanished. As the reality of prolonged remote work set in, I struggled profoundly in transitioning my sales approach to be effective on virtual platforms. My video calls felt stiff and reactive compared to the organic conversations I could drive sitting side by side prospects.

Like many salespeople anchored in old norms, I grappled to convey the same passion through a screen. However, adapting quickly became business critical. By reframing how I make personal connections digitally, ensure clarity in written communications, and leverage collaborative tools like shared screens, I ultimately forged a new virtual sales groove that kept momentum going. Now with hybrid policies cementing virtual buyer interactions as standard practice, mastering those onscreen sales skills has become essential for anyone hoping to hit their quotas. Let me walk you through exactly how I evolved my sales style over months of trial-and-error to thrive in the new virtual landscape we're all now operating in.

Remote selling via video conferencing is now imperative for sales teams. While in-person meetings still seal many large deals, buyers expect robust digital interaction options. Skilled presentation and rapport-building over video drives conversions and customer satisfaction much like face-to-face without the hassles of travel.

Keys for Impactful Video Sales Meetings

Successful virtual selling requires more than simply mimicking in-room interactions on-screen. The intimacy of webcams and potential distractions of attendees multi-tasking demand adaptations. These best practices create comfortable, professional video sales experiences:

- Send calendar invites with video calls embedded to simplify joining.
- Start sessions with casual conversation to build connections.
- Look directly into the camera to simulate eye contact.
- Speak slowly and clearly. Repeat key points for retention.
- Share slides and demos in presentation mode for easy viewing.
- Check frequently for reactions and questions.
- Keep meetings focused and fast paced.

Presenting Tips for Visual Learners

Sales guru Jeffrey Gitomer famously advised to "always be interesting." This proves even more important over video where drifting attention spans lower comprehension. Keep prospects engaged with compelling content tailored for on-screen delivery:

- Use large, uncluttered text and bold colors for slides.
- Embed relevant graphics and illustrations.
- Speak naturally as if telling a story vs. reading bullet points.
- Share camera view to present physical samples or prototypes.
- Annotate slides live with digital pen to emphasize areas.
- Play embedded animations and videos for multi-media dynamism.
- Use laser pointer tools to direct focus on charts or diagrams.

Interactive Demos Connect Virtual Audiences

Nothing substitutes for physical product demonstrations to show-case tangible differentiators and build visceral desire. Creative sales pros simulate this virtually via interactive walkthroughs audiences can partly direct themselves:

- Prepare customized demo scenarios for each prospect.
- Create modular demo elements to adapt to real-time feedback.
- Prompt attendees to choose demo directions or sample use cases.
- Encourage attendees to provide sample data inputs to process.
- Add floating chat windows so teams can exchange feedback in real time during demos.
- Email recordings post-meeting for sharing or review.

While screensharing applications enable remote collaboration nearly on par with in-person now, selling over video retains nuances beyond simply reproducing live settings digitally. Sales professionals investing effort to finely tune virtual sales techniques gain a distinct competitive advantage as location constraints evaporate in the modern commercial landscape.

While in-person deal closing retains advantages, buyers now expect robust digital sales interactions and presentations. Mastering video and virtual collaboration platforms has become essential for sales success. By focusing on building connections, maximizing retention with compelling content tailored for screens, and crafting interactive demos, sales professionals can replicate the tangible buyer experiences that drive conversions even over video calls. Invest time tuning your virtual sales techniques, from perfecting your on-camera presence to prompting live feedback during custom demos, and your results will thrive even as location constraints evaporate in the new digitally driven commercial landscape.

Chapter Ten - Data Analytics Optimization

When I first moved into a sales leadership role years ago, I'll admit - I was old school. Company hierarchy was the driving focus of culture. Rules ruled the day. You showed up early, did what you were told, never questioned authority, and stayed in the office till your work was complete. Gut instinct and experience when evaluating teams and performance was valued. But the game has shifted rapidly. As we usher in 2024 in an increasingly volatile market, it's impossible to achieve sustained success without tapping real-time data analytics. I learned this the hard way after a couple quarters of lagging forecasts last year.

Rather than writing it off as poor performance, I worked cross-functionally to implement a new cloud-based analytics platform. The instant visibility I gained into granular trends, from sales cycle duration down to content engagement, was a total wake-up call. I discovered stalled deals were stuck in contract phase while the blog content driving our leads failed to resonate. Armed with these actionable insights, I right-sized pipelines, implemented targeted content strategies, and optimized messaging for each customer tier.

Within two quarters of rallying my teams around the data, we exceeded all growth goals. I'm now a true believer in leveraging analytics to inform sales optimization. Selling based solely on legacy instincts without data science is no longer enough. As leaders, embracing platforms that centralize CRM, email, and content metrics provides the visibility needed to pinpoint priorities. Making data analysis core to strategy is key to scaling revenue in an increasingly competitive climate. Consider this your nudge to catch up to the future. Trust me, I learned the hard way just how game-changing analytics investment can be.

Advanced sales teams now rely extensively on data analytics and business intelligence to inform their strategies and operations. Quantifiable metrics drive precise assessments of pipeline health and forecast accuracy as well as optimal resource allocation. Granular visibility into conversion performance also fuels data-backed process improvements.

Moving From Reactive to Predictive Planning

In the past, sales leaders relied heavily on gut instinct and reactive tactics to hit targets. But lightning-fast business environments full of disruptions make interior data analytics foundational to resilient operations. Dynamic reporting converts hindsight into foresight across the organization, enabling predictive responses that keep revenue on track through turbulence. As a salesperson, it is critical to understand the new expectations and the advanced tools in play by leaders, managers, and companies.

Instrumenting Funnel Stage Progression

While managers once checked basic funnel metrics in aggregate occasionally, modern CRM analytics provide drillable visibility into specific stage progression rates. Where exactly do leads stagnate? Which stages underperform on conversion benchmarks? Do opportunities route most efficiently to best-match reps? Funnel analytics illuminates action areas.

Dynamically Optimizing Processes

End user behavior data informs iterative testing and versioning of sales processes to optimize efficiencies. If demos consistently lose prospects at certain sections, product marketers dig into usage analytics on those areas to shorten and enhance. Low email open or link click through rates prompt testing alternate outreach timing, copy, or creative approaches.

Essential Sales Metrics and KPIs (Key Performance indicators) to Instrument
- Lead Velocity: Average time from lead to customer
- Share of marketing qualified leads becoming sales qualified
- Prospect Engagement: Email opens, downloads, site visits
- Lead Quality: Conversion rates by lead source
- Sales Cycle Length: Average time from SQL to closed deal
- Average Deal Size: Bookings per contract stratified by segment
- ASP: Average annual contract value per customer
- Churn/Expansion: Upsells and renewals vs cancellations
- Funnel Stage Conversion Rates: Progression benchmarks from lead through proposal
- Win Rate: Share of proposals culminating in closed/won deals

With exponential data generation across business, sales teams ignoring insights risk flying blind while competitors execute strategically. Leaders as well as salespeople must make analytics optimization central to sales excellence now and into the future.

Chapter Eleven - Adapting Your Sales Mindset to Thrive Through Change

If you told my 25-year-old newbie sales rep self that one day I'd enthusiastically welcome seismic industry changes that uproot my entire approach, I would have called you crazy. I remember the long days pounding the pavement back then just hoping to hit quota relying on the old school tactics I had honed. Cold calls, PowerPoint demos stacked with product features, wining-and-dining every client contact – that was my solid playbook. So as technology and buying behavior rapidly advanced over the years, forcing adaptation became my worst nightmare. The introverted paper-filter in me despised re-learning new CRMs, social media platforms and virtual communication styles every 6 months.

However, after losing major deals due to competitors with cutting-edge solutions, I reached an inflection point. I knew burying my head to avoid confronting change was no longer sustainable if I wanted to remain solvent and relevant in sales. Though intensely uncomfortable, embracing trial-and-error around unfamiliar tools and tactics reinvigorated my career. Now over a decade later as both an individual sales leader AND guiding my teams through exponential market shifts, change adaptation has become my superpower. Whether the next inevitable disruption revolves around AI automation, augmented reality or who knows what, by constantly challenging my own mindset I'm now in a place to ride the wave.

Now when facing the swells of change headed our way in 2024 and beyond, remember– progress depends on first letting go of what made you successful before. My tale of reluctantly shedding old methods to ultimately elevate performance is one every seller must internalize to thrive amidst endless uncertainty.

Sales roles demand sharp resilience against inevitable rejection, disappointment, and unpredictable obstacles. But accelerating business transformation now pressures professionals to evolve mental reflexes just to sustain performance expectations, let alone set new benchmarks for exceptional. Growth oriented psychologies and self-care separate thriving teams from the stagnant.

Cultivating a Dynamic Growth Mindset

Fixed mindsets assume abilities as static - either you have innate sales talents or don't. But growth-oriented mindsets understand skills continuously improve through deliberate practice. Top producers view challenges as less intimidating, recasting obstacles as teachers on the journey to sales excellence over destinations. They interrogate losses for instructive patterns instead of accepting temporary defeats as destiny.

Getting Creative to Power Persistence

Inevitable setbacks chip away at motivation essential to push through the ups and downs of complex sales. Beating resignation back before it becomes burnout requires resourcefulness - trying ever-new tactics with an experimental ethos versus repetitive approaches bringing diminishing returns through change. Timely creativity levers both process innovations and psychological boosts to stay in dynamic growth mode.

Balancing Intensity with Stillness

Successfully riding sales turbulence long-term further relies on vigilant self-care counterbalancing demanding exertion required. Regular movement, stress mitigation practices like mindfulness or meditation, together with small breaks for broader perspective reset runaway cortisol and anxiety from 24/7 competitive environments.

Peak performance fusion channels intense effort and restorative renewal in equal measure - physically, emotionally, and mentally.

The quickening pace of change across business eliminates room for sales professionals wedded to static abilities or routines. But dynamically growing into new challenges through persistence-boosting creativity and intentional balancing of intensity with stillness sustains excellence amid chaos.

Sales has always required resilience and mental toughness to power through the inevitable rejections and obstacles. But the quickening pace of technological, economic, and social change now demands even greater mental agility and self-care from sales professionals striving to remain relevant and energized. Staying laser focused on personal growth unlocks rare persistence, creativity, and motivation to excel.

Embracing a Growth Mindset

Fixed mindsets believe abilities are static and effort bears little results. But growth-oriented mindsets realize skills can continually improve through dedication and creative strategies. Top performers view challenges as opportunities to build grit and expand capabilities. They analyze losses for lessons instead of accepting defeat.

Creativity Powers Persistence

Hitting walls of customer indifference or lost deals drains optimism over time. Countering this slide toward resignation demands resourcefulness exploring ever-new tactics with an experimental ethos. Leverage tools like creative brainstorming and design thinking to inject fresh approaches continually.

Beating Burnout Through Balance

The non-stop change sweeping sales inevitably fuels stress, anxiety, and burnout without vigilant self-care. Physical health, focused relaxation or meditation, and small breaks to reset perspective keep motivation high. Renewal sustains the enthusiasm and mental flexibility change accommodation requires.

Ultimately, selling evolves too rapidly now for professionals unwilling to iterate habits and mindsets. Letting the psychological weight of constant change accumulate slowly rigidifies thinking. But those learning to flex with the turbulence through growth, creativity, resilience tactics and balance discover new potentials amid the chaos - along with sustainable high performance.

Chapter Twelve – increase your thirst for Learning

I still vividly recall the wake-up call I received a few years ago in my commercial banking sales career. I prided myself on deep relationships with my initial client portfolio - having guided them from stagnate growth to rapid growth trajectories. Yet as their needs scaled into complex mergers, equity events and global expansion, I felt in over my head on financial options. Meanwhile, nimble fintech competitors carved out segments of our historical customers through tailored digital solutions my bank was still racing to develop.

My tried and true relationship-building approach no longer ensured value. And with banking innovation accelerating exponentially, I risked losing relevance without upskilling quick. Rather than pointing fingers at our bank's slow product development, I took ownership of reskilling personally including self-funded edtech courses on emerging practice areas.

Then when chatting with next gen bankers clinging to traditional relationship selling, I emphasize – hybrid digital and human trust is the future. Continuous learning helps me merge old school consultative banking with new school speed and technology. It's challenging perpetually upskilling but ultimately the formula to dominate across embedded and emerging client needs amid constant fintech disruption. Equip yourself for the long learning marathon ahead! Continuous Learning - The New Imperative for Sales Pros

The rapid digitization and constant change in the sales landscape demands that reps commit to continuous learning just to keep pace. The playbooks, tactics and even products we sell evolve so quickly that resting on past success is a recipe for rapid irrelevance. Top performers across industries amplify their skills through structured self-education to build sustainable excellence amid shifting seller requirements.

Actions to Cultivate Your Learning Practice

Conduct an Annual Sales Skills Audit

Be ruthlessly honest evaluating current proficiency across different sales competencies from product expertise to consultative questioning abilities. Identify strength areas to double down on and gaps needing development. Refresh this audit every 6-12 months as a learning checkpoint.

Curate Your Personal Development Resources

Subscribe to sales podcasts and short-form video training platforms that align to your growth goals. Join industry forums to exchange ideas with peers. Set a monthly time allowance for self-guided enrichment based on audit findings. Consider working with a sales coach for tailored guidance.

Direct Your Own Learning Journey

Catalog personal education resources and formal training opportunities in an individual development plan. Align activities to your strengths, interests and growth objectives. Managers guide this journey not prescribe it.

Continuous skills elevation through self-directed learning is the new imperative for salespeople to sustain excellence. Frequent self-audits, curated education resources and defined development plans let reps adapt to constant change.

Staying Ahead of the Curve Through Lifelong Learning

The sales landscape evolves rapidly - new technologies emerge, buyer behaviors shift, and fresh competitors arise. Top performers must commit to ongoing education to continually adapt their skills and knowledge.

Rather than viewing learning as a one-time event or periodic requirement, embrace continuous growth as a lifelong mindset. Dedicate time weekly to enrich your expertise. Seek out perspectives beyond your immediate role to expand thinking. Leverage modern formats like microlearning and social selling mentors to integrate development into daily workflows.

Strive to lead change in your industry instead of merely reacting to it. Pursue emerging best practices before managers mandate adoption. Pilot new sales technologies long before formal rollout in your organization. Frame your curiosity as an asset to position yourself as a visionary leader.

As Eric Hoffer famously stated, "In a time of drastic change it is the learners who inherit the future. The learned usually find themselves equipped to live in a world that no longer exists."

Commit now to lifelong learning so you remain equipped to excel in the sales world of tomorrow. Pursue mastery across both prevailing and emerging competencies. Make continuous elevation of your skills, knowledge and capabilities a core element of your personal brand and sales DNA.

The future of selling will only grow more complex and fast-changing. But for sales professionals passionate about perpetual growth and committed to staying ahead of the curve through constant learning - an exciting road lies ahead.

Chapter Thirteen - Preparing Sales Strategies for What's Next

When I started in commercial lending sales years ago, relationships were everything. My ability to gain the deep trust through face-to-face talks with business owners ensured consistent deal flow. Though over many cycles my approach remained consistent, the market landscape shifted dramatically beneath me. Digital banks armed with sophisticated data analytics threatened longstanding loyalties.

I wrongly doubled down on old-school insights over modern tech-enabled understanding of client needs. In several painful quarters, I saw critical wholesale customers switch to more predictive competitors I once dismissed.

I faced a choice between clinging to an outdated relational selling philosophy or aggressively upgrading digital skillsets to stay valuable. I threw my weight into studying web design, optimizing online content, analyzing website client behavior through AI tools to reinvent consultative connections.

Now that I am again in direct sales for commercial insurance, I emphasize that genuine partnership today means fluidly meshing high tech capabilities like cashflow projections with high-touch guidance through pivotal moments. Relying on the past guarantees extinction. Committing to perpetual skills elevation around emerging fintech is the only path to deliver complete value to wholesale clients as environments evolve. Keep attacking your learning edge!

Here are some key tasks I would include in a chapter on preparing sales strategies for the future:

- Assess the Competitive Landscape - Research digital solutions from insurtech competitors and where they're gaining traction
- Identify Emerging Customer Needs - Survey clients on desired improvements in coverage, service, communication etc.
- Map the Modern Buyer's Journey - Outline touchpoints and pain points across discovering, evaluating and purchasing insurance
- Audit Your Tech-Enabled Capabilities - Review abilities across video sales, online analytics, digital engagement tools, and AI to identify gaps
- Define Key Future-Focused Sales Competencies - Determine new skills needed to advise clients using data insights, digital efficiency etc.
- Craft Personalized Development Plans - Create plans to close high priority skills gaps through training, certifications etc.
- Pilot New Sales Tech and Approaches - Test updated techniques focused on customization and tech fluency with select accounts
- Measure Effectiveness - Evaluate pilot KPIs including deal velocity, expanded services per client, retention rates
- Refine Successful Innovations - Integrate top performing digital sales process changes into standard model
- Commit to Continuous Improvement - Schedule quarterly reviews to realign strategies to market evolution and upgrade capabilities

As we enter 2024, I remind up-and-coming direct sellers that perpetual skills elevation enables delivering value amid constant tech-fueled change. Whether innovating video sales techniques through TikTok or optimizing online funnel metrics via AI tools, learning agility separates thriving reps from stagnating ones.

Specific actions I prioritize quarterly include assessing the latest virtual sales tech through market reports, evaluating my personal KPIs against benchmarks, and dedicating monthly self-study time to sharpen my digital toolset. Committing to continuous skills upgrading ensures I engage modern buyers on their terms no matter how direct pipelines evolve. Adaptability is oxygen.

Chapter Fourteen - Thriving Through Disruption: Cultivating an Agile Sales Mindset

I've witnessed tremendous change across my 35-year sales career from mainframe computers to mobile devices, analog calls to digital engagement, basic CRMs to advanced analytics. The acceleration of technological innovation guarantees even more change ahead.

Sales professionals must cultivate an agile mindset and adaptable skillset to thrive amid constant disruption. This means welcoming change versus resisting it, making incremental improvements based on feedback, and remaining nimble in the face uncertainty.

Core Tenets of an Agile Selling Mindset

Flexible Thinking
Approach innovation opportunities with an open mind rather than clinging to past models. View change as a chance to improve.

Comfort with Uncertainty - Ambiguity sparks creativity. Leverage scenario planning to map possibilities instead of predicting singular outcomes.

Test and Learn Orientation - Design small experiments to validate new concepts before wide rollout. Use measured pilots to guide refinement.

Focus on Continuous Improvement - Collect regular feedback via customer advisory boards. Set quarterly skills development objectives.

Cross-Functional Collaboration - Work jointly with tech teams to complement AI capabilities with human strengths.

Ongoing Skills Development - The shelf-life of specific sales tactics and tools shortens yearly. Maintain an insatiable appetite to learn emerging methods.

Key Ways to Stay Adaptable
*   Immerse in Innovation Forums - Attend conferences and events focused on sales transformation trends. Connect with peers pioneering new models.
*   Pilot New Tools - Test cutting-edge sales tech with subsets of customers to determine effectiveness before large investments.
*   Develop Agile Leadership - Cultivate versatility across both field sales and digital roles. Pursue lateral moves to broaden capabilities.
*   Master In-Demand Skills - Develop competencies like virtual presentation delivery, data analytics, and social selling.

While technologies will continuously evolve, human judgment, emotional intelligence and consultation skills remain pivotal for sales excellence. Anchor in these timeless abilities while continually adapting to capitalize on emerging innovations.

Agility separates future-ready sales teams while rigidness leads to irrelevance. Make continuous improvements guided by real-world experiments and feedback. Maintain an adaptable mindset to ultimately turn disruption into competitive advantage.

Building a Future-Proof Sales Function

The question facing sales leaders today is not if the next wave of disruption is coming but how rapidly it will arrive and transform buying expectations. Customer needs, market offerings, and selling models will inevitably look starkly different in just a few years.

Sales organizations must build institutional muscle to flex with the times instead of stubbornly clinging to what worked previously. Construct structures using cross-functional teams over rigid hierarchies, for example, to enable responsiveness. Implement modular technology architectures to plug in new tools as needed. Maintain a perpetual test-and-learn mindset open to adjustments.

Most importantly, develop key leaders and personnel who embody the agile and adaptable traits outlined in this chapter. Instill resilience across the entire revenue engine to thrive through whatever change emerges on the horizon.

The job of transforming a sales function is never done as disruption and improvement exist in a virtuous cycle. But frequently inspecting your operating system for flexibility bottlenecks is the best way to catch impediments before they catch you.

The future will accelerate toward us shortly - meet it with boldness instead of bracing for impact. An agile sales function stands ready to capitalize on change rather than being victimized by it. Now let's get to work.

Chapter Fifteen - Double Down on Customer Experience

In an increasingly commoditized marketplace, customer experience (CX) has become the key sustainable competitive advantage for companies. Sales teams play a crucial role in driving CX by truly understanding and advocating for customers across the organization. Stand out by doubling down on CX using these approaches:

Hyper-Focus On Customer Needs and Pain Points and solutions

The fastest way to improve CX is addressing your customers' biggest struggles. Make pain point relief your obsession – they will love you for it. Dig deep into customer needs by:
- Spending more discovery call time on problem interrogation
- Creating customer journey maps to expose friction spots.
- Surveying users about challenges through polls and questionnaires
- Interviewing churned customers to understand why they left.

Master their unmet needs, then perfectly position how you solve them. Customers will flock to you.

Provide Omnichannel Purchasing Experiences

Give your customers flexible options to research, purchase from, and engage with you. Meet them wherever they are by enabling:
- Shopping across desktop and mobile responsive sites
- Buying through reps, retail stores, resellers - whatever they prefer
- Switching seamlessly between channels without repeating steps
- Engaging via phone, email, chat, SMS, social media and more

The more frictionless paths available, the more revenue you generate.

Leverage User Reviews and Feedback Loops

Reviews have become the lifeblood of purchase decisions. Encourage happy customers to leave positive ratings and leverage constructive feedback to fuel constant improvement. Strategies include:
- Sending review requests soon after positive interactions
- Monitoring review sites to promptly address concerns.
- Surveying users to solicit product enhancement ideas.
- Sharing updates and changes driven by user input

This closed-loop system tells customers they are heard while capturing insights to build better experiences.

By removing obstacles and aligning completely to "jobs to be done", you make the buying process joyful. That earns their loyalty for life.

Here is a draft conclusion to the chapter on doubling down on customer experience for sales professionals:

Creating Standout Experiences for Enduring Loyalty

In an increasingly noisy and undifferentiated market, customer experience reigns supreme. Sales teams must champion the customer within organizations to drive positive engagement across the buyer's journey.

Rather than treating CX as a one-off initiative, embed it into the fabric of your culture. Establish standalone CX metrics and goals beyond lagging measures of revenue and conversions alone. Celebrate wins that strengthen lifetime loyalty as much as short-term sales figures.

Structure reverse mentorships where junior customer-facing team members advise senior leaders on emerging pain points. Formalize customer advisory boards to guide your roadmap. Empower support and success teams to capture insights that feed improvement.

By continually realigning around the customer, you produce standout experiences that turn one-time buyers into enthusiastic advocates. This community of brand ambassadors fuels sustainable growth through referrals and increased wallet share over time.

The future of sales growth lies in doubling down on customer-centricity today. Make it your personal mission to know buyers better than they know themselves through relentless empathy and dedication to their needs first. Remove friction wherever it manifests to spark delight. Deliver for the customer and the customer will deliver for your business.

Chapter Sixteen - Create Your Niche

After spending 35 years in Commercial Banking for a few major commercial banks, I'd mastered the art of complex debt products. My intricate knowledge and expertise analyzing risk. Rattling off bank leverage ratios and credit risks flowed naturally as breathing. I lived and breathed complex lending, treasury, and LIBOR rates.

When leadership reshuffled our commercial segment, I faced a stark choice: relearn middle-market lending from scratch or leave banking entirely. The thought of abandoning a thriving career terrified me but starting back at page one after so much specialization felt equally daunting. However in a leap of faith, I have pivoted into Commercial insurance sales – and found my niche. All the custom product structuring and client advisory skills I honed in risk management proved invaluable again, albeit for Main Street merchants versus Wall Street execs. Now instead of relying on industry tenure, each day I get to flex my expertise muscle crafting tailored solutions.

They say you can't teach an old dog new tricks but this ex-banker will adamantly tell you otherwise. Whether shifting sectors or starting afresh, embracing the uncertainty of 're-specializing' can unlock your next level of success. I'm proof you simply need the guts to make your leap!

The days of being a generalist seller across all products and industries have passed. To excel today, smart salespeople niche down into a focused vertical industry or buyer persona to become domain experts. Specializing establishes credibility, helps you hyper-target prospects, and lets you provide genuine value. Follow these best practices to specialize effectively:

Become a Vertical Industry Expert

Rather than spreading yourself thinly across many sectors, double down on truly mastering one industry such as tech, manufacturing, healthcare, or finance. Vertical expertise wins business by understanding a prospect's world view. Gain insider knowledge by:

- Reading industry publications, blogs, and analyst reports voraciously
- Learning industry terminology until it's second nature
- Understanding the competitive landscape and key players
- Speaking at vertical conferences to build your brand

When you can discuss accounts' pain points or emerging trends better than they can, you position yourself as an essential advisor.

Curate Niche Content to Attract Your Ideal Customers

Digital marketing has made niche targeting extremely powerful. You can now reach your perfect prospects at scale. Become a hub for niche content that appeals specifically to your vertical. Tactics include:

- Writing and promoting vertical-specific eBooks, whitepapers and blog posts
- Creating a niche newsletter or podcast sharing insider tips
- Hosting webinars featuring vertical guest experts
- Building a segmented prospect list for content promotion

This niche content draws qualified visitors for high-quality lead gen.

Participate in Relevant Online Communities

Your specialized expertise should make you a fixture in related online communities. Participate frequently by:
- Joining and engaging in niche Slack/Discord channels
- Contributing high-value posts to vertical forums and groups
- Commenting on industry discussions across Twitter and LinkedIn
- Guest writing for vertical publications

Help solve problems and provide guidance without overly 'selling'. Becoming a trusted member of these communities leads to referrals and warm introductions.

In competitive markets, expertise creates competitive advantage. Specializing makes sales a high-value, consultative profession again. Determine the niche you're most passionate about then earn your stripes as a true vertical expert.

The days of generalist sellers are over in the modern market. As this chapter has explored, taking a specialized approach focused on a specific vertical, buyer persona or product niche is now essential to sales success.

By becoming true subject matter experts in a focused area, salespeople build instant credibility and convey genuine value to customers and prospects. Specializing allows you to talk prospects' language, hyper-target content, and provide tailored solutions specific to each account's needs.

While abandoning comfortable breadth for intense specialization can feel intimidating at first, ultimately it unlocks new levels of high-impact, consultative selling. Choose your niche area passionately, dive deeply into insider knowledge, and actively participate in related communities.

When you can discuss accounts' pain points even better than they can themselves, you have truly earned your stripes as an indispensable advisor. In an increasingly competitive world, expertise stands alone. It's time to niche down and realize your full potential as a specialized sales pro at the top of their game.

Chapter Seventeen - Expand Your Skillset

After building deep relationships in the banking industry for over a decade, I thought I had sales figured out. My pitches were polished, my connections were solid, and I could secure deals in my sleep. Complacency started to creep in as the years went by - why fix what isn't broken? However, the industry and the business world had other plans.

Many of my loyal long-term bank customers suddenly started moving to nonbank competitors offering cutting-edge digital solutions and machine learning analytics that I could hardly comprehend. Instead of panicking or admitting defeat, this inflection point lit a fire under me. I realized that no matter your tenure or past successes, staying competitive requires continuously expanding your skills.

I threw myself into learning our bank's new digital platforms and AI capabilities. I completely revamped my sales collateral and pitches to highlight these advanced offerings. I also proactively contacted accounts at risk of attrition, demonstrating how our innovative tools could better meet their changing needs. After an intense quarter of internal training and getting up to speed on services I had little exposure to just months earlier, I not only retained the vast majority of customers but closed two major upsell deals leveraging new tools I had yet to fully master.

While difficult at times, resisting complacency and continually learning - whether about emerging technologies or evolving customer behaviors - is the only way to thrive in the fast-paced banking industry long-term. The sales game only accelerates, so as banking professionals we must all commit to aggressively expand our skill sets regardless of tenure or specialization. Consider this your nudge to step outside your comfort zone and level up!

The sales landscape is shifting rapidly. While the core values of selling remain constant - solving customer problems, building relationships, closing deals - the methods, tools, and skills needed to succeed are evolving quicker than ever. Salespeople who rest on traditional tactics will quickly fall behind the curve. To thrive in modern sales, you must expand your skillset across three key areas: consultative selling, customer experience, and virtual selling.

Consultative Selling Skills

Transactional selling focused purely on exchanging product for money is dying. The salespeople who will thrive are those who provide real value and insights before the sale. You must enhance your consultative selling abilities by:

- Asking probing questions to deeply understand customer goals, challenges, and processes
- Identifying hidden customer needs they may not realize themselves
- Providing unique perspectives and advice beyond what your product solves
- Presenting multiple solutions suited to different user personas and use cases
- Helping customers arrive at the buying decision, not pushing them there

These consultative skills demonstrate you can provide strategic value beyond taking orders. Customers will come to rely on your expertise.

Customer Experience Skills

With the explosion of consumer choice, customer experience is emerging as the key differentiator between vendors. To stand out, double down on CX by:

- Obsessing over removing any point of friction for users
- Optimizing self-service options and educational resources
- Closing experience gaps across pre-sales, sales, and post-sales
- Gathering and acting on Voice-of-Customer feedback
- Collaborating across departments to improve end-to-end journeys

Enhancing CX boosts sales by making your offering easier to buy, use, and renew.

Virtual Selling Capabilities

Selling has gone fully remote. Sales cycles from first call to closed deal increasingly happen over video conferences and phone without in-person meetings. Step up your virtual selling game by:

- Mastering online sales tools like Zoom, Gong, Outreach, and Slack
- Refining your personal video sales room setup for credibility
- Adapting your pitching style and materials for remote delivery
- Leveraging screensharing and remote demos to showcase value
- Developing SMS, chat, and email outreach strategies

Get completely comfortable selling through a screen. Clients expect nothing less in our digital world.

Continuous Learning Mindset

Ultimately, sales is a knowledge profession. To build this versatile skillset, dedicate yourself to being a lifelong learner by:
- Reading sales books and publications during your commute
- Listening to sales podcasts and audiobooks at the gym
- Signing up for useful online sales courses
- Attending virtual conferences and webinars
- Joining a mentorship program at your company

Carving out an hour every day for focused learning compounds over years into a tremendous advantage your competitors will struggle to match.

The salesperson with the most diverse and modern skillset wins. Expand your capabilities across consultative selling, customer experience, and virtual selling fluency. Back it all with a growth mindset focused on mastery. By becoming a Swiss Army knife of seller skills, no opportunity can resist you!

The sales landscape is shifting under our feet. While the core values of problem-solving and relationship-building remain steady, the specific skills and methods required to drive results are evolving faster than ever.

As this chapter has demonstrated, sales professionals must continuously expand their capabilities across three pivotal areas — consultative selling, customer experience, and virtual selling fluency. Enhancing your strategic advisory chops, optimizing end-to-end CX, and selling seamlessly through screens are now baseline requirements to stay ahead.

Underpinning it all is cultivating a growth mindset focused on life-long learning. Carve out time every single day to level up through books, podcasts, courses and mentors. Compound knowledge into an unbeatable edge.

The salesperson with the most modern and diverse skill set wins in the end. Become that versatile Swiss Army knife seller able to toggle approaches on demand. Don't let your dated tactics hold you back another day from dominating your market. Expand your skills immediately and unlock new levels of sales success.

My Concluding Thoughts - Adaptation is the New Normal

Across these seventeen chapters, a central theme emerges around sales roles rapidly evolving amid mounting technological, economic, and social change. Where once professionals could rest on predictable approaches, the pace of innovation now demands flexibility, growth mindsets, and capability building as a way of life to stay competitive.

Key lessons repeat across areas:

Leverage Technology but Remain Human-Centered

As datasets, algorithms, and smart tools empower sales teams to hyper-personalize, operate smarter, and automate repetitive tasks, the human skills of listening, strategic questioning, relationship building and creative problem solving become more pivotal - and rare. Blend cutting-edge tech with emotional intelligence for outsized results.

Specialize and Consult, Don't Just Sell

Commoditization means selling generic products on feature checklists alone fails. Salespeople must niche down as vertical experts addressing specific pain points, then guide customers in advisory partnerships beyond transactions. This earns trust and loyalty amid mounting options.

Obsess Over Customer Experience

With self-service sales proliferating across digital channels, human reps differentiate by removing obstacles and aligning organizations around customer needs. This means advocating beyond sales silos to optimize end-to-end journeys. First call resolution and frictionless buying is the future.

Master Both In-Person and Virtual Selling

For the foreseeable future, complex B2B sales combine physical and digital interactions. Adaptable sales professionals finesse online tools like video conferencing and sales engagement software to remote pitches while retaining in-person relationship building for local prospects when useful. This omnichannel versatility ensures relevance.

Grow Your Skills and Perspectives Constantly

Finally, selling must become a profession of lifelong learning rather than fixed expertise given rapid environmental changes. Consume books, podcasts, courses and webinars continually while synthesizing insights across domains. This fluid growth sustains performance amid fluid conditions.

While specific tactics constantly evolve across modern sales functions, these underlying imperatives for adaptability, customer-centricity, specialization and constant learning equip professionals to ride whatever market changes loom ahead. By focusing less on specific playbooks and more on ever-expanding skills and evolutionary mindsets, salespeople future-proof themselves to thrive through turbulence rather than becoming overwhelmed by change.

What futuristic innovations remain just over the horizon? What new competitor disruptions rock complacent teams? The answers surely surprise - but prepared, focused sales teams adept at flexibility, lifelong learning and resilience can turn even the most uncertainty into opportunity. The future remains bright for professionals embracing sales' new reality of constant adaptation!

Any lastly – do not forget that all relationships will always matter and that work-ethic will keep your edge against the fully life-balanced competitors. I had to end with the last "Old school" time tested differentiator I am holding on to for now.

Happy Selling!

Stuart Pattison is an accomplished sales leader with over 35 years of experience driving growth, revenue, and profitability in the banking and finance industries. He has held numerous executive positions including EVP, Regional Manager, President, and CEO for small and large companies.

Throughout his career, Stuart has developed and executed innovative sales strategies that exceeded targets and transformed underperforming banks into top market leaders. He is especially skilled at building high-performance teams, streamlining operations, championing mergers and acquisitions, and fostering cultures focused on client relationships.

Today, Stuart shares his sales, leadership, and management expertise through speaking, writing, and consulting. He aims to prepare sales professionals and teams for excelling in an increasingly complex and changing landscape.